The Countries

Hungary

Kristin Van Cleaf
ABDO Publishing Company

visit us at
www.abdopublishing.com

Published by ABDO Publishing Company, 8000 West 78th Street, Edina, Minnesota 55439.
Copyright © 2008 by Abdo Consulting Group, Inc. International copyrights reserved in all
countries. No part of this book may be reproduced in any form without written permission from the
publisher. The Checkerboard Library™ is a trademark and logo of ABDO Publishing Company.

Printed in the United States.

Interior Photos: Alamy pp. 6, 16, 18, 19, 24, 31; AP Images pp. 5, 12, 13, 21, 22, 23, 27, 33, 35;
    Corbis pp. 10, 26, 34, 36, 37; Getty Images pp. 9, 32; Peter Arnold p. 29

Editors: Tamara L. Britton, Megan M. Gunderson
Art Direction & Maps: Neil Klinepier

Library of Congress Cataloging-in-Publication Data

Van Cleaf, Kristin, 1976-
  Hungary / Kristin Van Cleaf.
      p. cm. -- (The countries)
  Includes index.
  ISBN 978-1-59928-783-6
  1. Hungary--Juvenile literature. I. Title.

  DB906.V326 2008
  943.9--dc22

                                                                    2007010180

Contents

Szervusztok!

Hello from Hungary! Hungary is a nation in central Europe. It lies in the ancient **basin** created by the famous Danube River.

Hungary is a beautiful land of plains, hills, and mountains. Its capital city, Budapest, sits on a wide maze of caves. Hot springs make the city's spas popular with tourists.

This country has struggled with invasions in its past. And, different governments made changes to Hungarian **culture**. As a result, many Hungarian traditions are no longer practiced.

But, Hungarians have endured through this hardship. Today, Hungary is a multicultural nation. It blends different ways of life from around the world to create a great place to work and live.

Szervusztok from Hungary!

Fast Facts

OFFICIAL NAME: Republic of Hungary
CAPITAL: Budapest

LAND
- Area: 35,919 square miles (93,030 sq km)
- Mountain Ranges: Bakony, Mátra
- Highest Point: Mount Kékes, 3,327 feet (1,014 m)
- Major Rivers: Tisza, Danube

PEOPLE
- Population: 9,956,108 (July 2007 estimate)
- Major Cities: Budapest, Debrecen, Miskolc
- Language: Hungarian (official)
- Religions: Roman Catholic, Calvinist Protestant, Lutheran, Greek Catholic

GOVERNMENT
- Form: Parliamentary democracy
- Head of State: President
- Head of Government: Prime minister
- Legislature: Unicameral National Assembly
- Nationhood: December 25, 1000

ECONOMY
- Agricultural Products: Wheat, corn, sunflower seeds, potatoes, beets, pigs, cattle, poultry, dairy products
- Mining Products: Coal, iron, oil, manganese, natural gas, bauxite
- Manufactured Products: Textiles, processed foods, chemicals, automobiles, metal products
- Money: Forint (1 forint = 100 fillers)

BUDAPEST

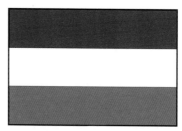

Hungary's flag

Hungarian forints

Timeline

896	Árpád leads Magyar tribes to settle present-day Hungary
1000	Stephen I is crowned king by Pope Sylvester II
1458	Matthias Corvinus becomes king
1526	The Ottoman Empire conquers Hungary
1686	Austria defeats the Ottomans and takes control of Hungary
1848	Lajos Kossuth leads a rebellion against Austria
1867	Austria-Hungary is created
1914	World War I begins
1919	The Treaty of Saint-Germain separates Hungary from Austria
1941	Hungary enters World War II
1945	Soviet-supported communist government gains control in Hungary
1956	Freedom Fighters stage an unsuccessful anti-Soviet uprising
1989	Communism ends in Europe
1990	Hungary elects a democratic government
1999	Hungary joins NATO
2004	Hungary joins the European Union

Hungary's History

In 896, Chief Árpád (AWR-pawd) and seven Magyar tribes entered present-day Hungary. They settled near the Danube River and conquered the Slavic tribes that lived there. Then, they began to seize surrounding territory.

In 972, Árpád's grandson Géza (GAY-zah) became chief. He united the Magyar tribes into a stronger nation. Géza's son Stephen continued this effort. In 1000, Pope Sylvester II crowned him King Stephen I.

Hungary prospered under King Stephen's rule. The nation remained strong until 1241. That year, Mongols invaded and killed nearly half of Hungary's people. When they withdrew, Hungary was destroyed.

In 1308, Charles I became king and restored order. His son Louis I gained control of surrounding lands. But after King Louis died, Hungary's leadership became weak. So, the **Ottoman Empire** began to invade Hungary.

Matthias Corvinus

In 1458, Matthias Corvinus became king. He protected the people from the **Ottomans**. King Matthias reformed the government and made the tax system more fair. He also supported the arts and founded a library.

But after his death, weak kings went back on King Matthias's reforms. The country's defenses were **depleted**. On August 29, 1526, the Ottomans finally conquered Hungary.

Central Hungary became part of the Ottoman Empire. In the east, Transylvania became an Ottoman **principality**. Austria claimed parts of western Hungary. This area was called Royal Hungary.

For a number of years, life in Hungary was difficult. Villages were destroyed, and people were killed or enslaved. In the late 1600s, the people in Royal Hungary **rebelled**. But, Austria quickly crushed the rebellion.

The Ottomans wanted to control all of Hungary. So in 1683, they attacked Austria. In 1686, Austria defeated the Ottoman Empire and took control of Hungary.

Under Austrian rule, many Austrians and Germans settled in Hungary. When Joseph II became Austria's king in 1780, he attempted to blend these **cultures**. He made German Hungary's official language.

But in the early 1800s, Hungary began a cultural renaissance. Hungarians embraced their history and traditions. And, two prominent men worked to achieve Hungarian independence.

István Széchenyi (SAY-chehn-yih) worked for **economic** developments such as new roads and bridges. And, he improved the Danube so that ships could sail all the way to the Black Sea. He was sure liberty would follow economic progress.

But Lajos Kossuth (KAW-shut) had different ideas about gaining independence. He believed that Hungary needed to be free of Austrian control. Only then could Hungarians have liberty.

In 1848, Kossuth led a **rebellion** against the government. Reforms called the March Laws were

Lajos Kossuth

granted. But in 1849, Austria put down the uprising. Kossuth fled the country.

However, the two sides began to work out an agreement. In 1867, the **dual** monarchy of Austria-Hungary was created. With this, Hungary finally became independent.

After independence, Hungary's industry and communications were modernized. But, the country still had some problems. As people moved to the cities for work, those areas became crowded.

There was also conflict between different **ethnic** groups who wanted independence from Austria-Hungary. To this end, Bosnian Serb Gavrilo Princip murdered Austria's Archduke Franz Ferdinand in June 1914. This started **World War I**.

Austria-Hungary took Germany's side in the war. But, many Hungarians thought the war served Austria and Germany's interests. And, they were inspired by the success of the **Russian Revolution**. So, they **rebelled** against the government and made Mihály Károlyi (KAW-rawl-yee) leader.

Austria-Hungary lost the war. But, in 1919, the Treaty of Saint-Germain made Austria and Hungary separate countries.

Hungary joined the **League of Nations** in 1922. However, the **Great Depression** soon brought worldwide **economic** failure.

In the 1930s, Adolf Hitler came to power in Germany. He planned to conquer other countries. In 1941, Hungary entered **World War II** on Germany's side. But in 1945, the Soviet Union invaded Hungary. Hungary lost the war.

After the war, the Soviet-supported **communist** party gained control of the government. By 1949, Hungary had a communist **constitution** and government led by Mátyás Rákosi (RAW-koh-shee).

On October 23, 1956, students called the Freedom Fighters staged an anti-Soviet uprising in Budapest. But,

Soviet forces stopped the **rebellion** in November.

In the 1960s, reforms helped the economy improve. However, economic growth slowed in the 1970s. Living standards dropped as a result.

The Freedom Fighters wave Hungary's flag over a captured Soviet tank.

In 1989, **communism** fell across Europe. Hungary's National Assembly revised its **constitution** and made the country a **democracy**. It passed laws to establish elections, guarantee people's rights, and create government structure. The Republic of Hungary was declared on October 23, 1989.

In 1990, the people elected a new democratic government. Throughout the next ten years, many social, **economic**, and political changes took place.

In 1999, Hungary joined **NATO**. The country joined the **European Union (EU)** in 2004. Today, Hungary continues to grow as a strong nation.

Fireworks explode over Buda Castle to celebrate Hungary's acceptance into the EU.

Mountains and Plains

Hungary is located in central Europe. Slovakia lies to the north. Ukraine lies to the northeast, and Romania is to the southeast. Serbia, Croatia, and Slovenia share Hungary's south and southwest borders. And, Austria lies to the west.

Most of the country is flat. But the Bakony and Mátra (MAH-trah) mountains run across the north central part of Hungary. Mount Kékes (KAY-kehs) is in the Mátra Mountains. At 3,327 feet (1,014 m), it is Hungary's highest peak.

The Danube is the country's main river. It divides Hungary in two. Margaret Island lies in the Danube. It is a garden-filled park, where swimming is popular with many Hungarians.

The Great Alföld (AWL-fuhld) lies east of the Danube. This low plain covers about half of the country. Because of its rich soil, most of Hungary's farms are in this area. There, water from the Tisza River **irrigates** the crops.

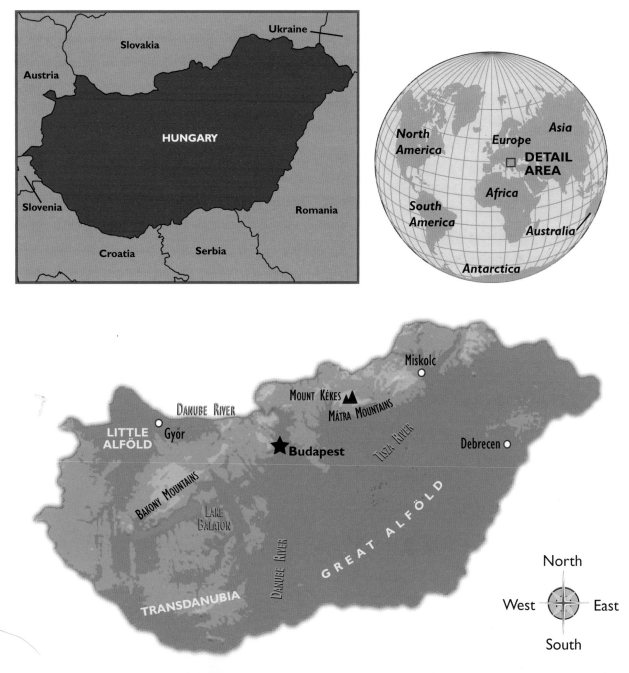

West of the Danube is Transdanubia. This area is a mix of hills and **highlands**. Lake Balaton is located there. At 231 square miles (598 sq km), it is central Europe's largest freshwater lake.

In northwestern Hungary is a pocket of plains surrounded by mountains. It is called the Little Alföld. Like the Great Alföld, it is a farming region.

Hungary's climate is fairly dry. The plains receive about 20 inches (50 cm) of rain in a year. An average of 30 inches (75 cm) of rain falls in the mountains. In summer, it is usually about 68 degrees Fahrenheit (20°C). Winter is cold and cloudy, with little snow. In winter, it is about 36 degrees Fahrenheit (2°C).

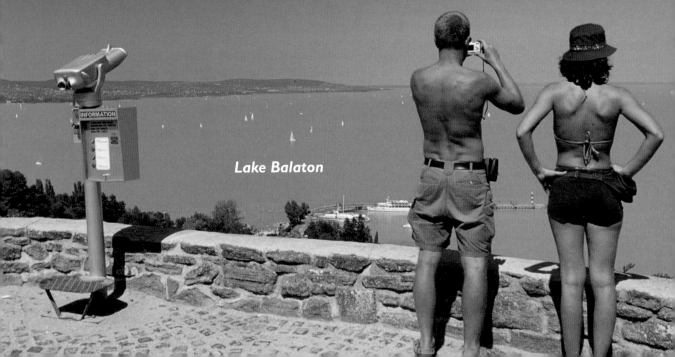

Lake Balaton

Rainfall

AVERAGE YEARLY RAINFALL

Inches		Centimeters
Under 20	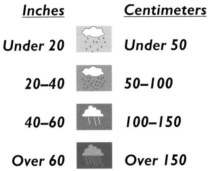	Under 50
20–40		50–100
40–60		100–150
Over 60		Over 150

Temperature

AVERAGE TEMPERATURE

Fahrenheit		Celsius
Over 65°		Over 18°
54°–65°		12°–18°
43°–54°		6°–12°
32°–43°		0°–6°
21°–32°		-6°–0°
Below 21°		Below -6°

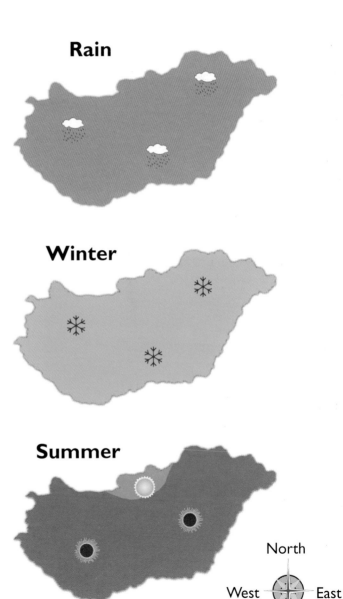

Rain

Winter

Summer

North

West — East

South

Plants and Animals

Today, only about one-third of Hungary's land remains meadow, pasture, forest, and woodland. The remaining land is used for agriculture and human settlement. This has caused many animals to lose their natural **habitats**.

But, there are still some wild places where animals live. Animals such as wild boars, roe deers, and foxes make their homes in Hungary's mountain forests. Beech trees grow in the higher elevations. On the lower slopes, oak trees are more common.

Black storks build their nests in forest trees and eat mostly freshwater fish.

Grasses grow in Hungary's meadows and pastures. Here, distinctive flowers include wild peonies, hellebores, pheasant's eyes, meadow anemones, and sages. Pheasants, quails, partridges, and rabbits also live in these areas. Swallows and the distinctive black storks **migrate** here in the summer.

Bustards are one of the heaviest flying birds. They can weigh up to 46 pounds (21 kg)!

Hungary's rivers and lakes are home to many fish. Wels catfish, pike, eels, and carp are common. Waterbirds such as avocets, stilts, and egrets enjoy these wet **habitats**, too. But, bustards like to stay on dry land!

Hungarians are working to protect their remaining plants and animals. They have created nine national parks and many conservation areas. In total, the government protects 3,151 square miles (8,161 sq km) of land.

Republic of Hungary

In the past, Hungary has had many different types of government. But in 1989, the people created a **parliamentary democracy**. Today, all citizens who are at least 18 years old may vote to choose their country's leaders.

Hungary has a one-house **parliament** called the National Assembly. Its 386 members are elected every four years. They have the power to **debate** and pass laws.

The National Assembly elects the president to a five-year term. It also elects the prime minister. And, it chooses the Council of Ministers, which the prime minister leads. The ministers lead various government departments.

Hungary's judicial branch is run by the **Constitutional** Court. It reviews laws to make sure they follow the constitution. This court has 11 seats elected to nine-year terms by the National Assembly. Below this court are courts of appeals, county courts, and local courts.

Locally, Hungary is divided into 19 counties. As the capital, Budapest is divided into 27 districts. Local governments are responsible for local transportation, utilities, and security. They are also in charge of **economic**, social, and **cultural** activities, as well as care for the **environment**.

Hungary's parliament building sits on the banks of the Danube River in Budapest. It took 17 years to build and contains 40 million bricks!

Hungarians

Most of Hungary's people are Hungarian. Some citizens are Roma peoples. They speak Hungarian, the country's official language.

Hungarians are free to choose their religion. Two-thirds of the people are Roman Catholic. Some are Calvinist **Protestants**. Others practice Lutheran or Greek Catholic faiths. And, some practice no religion.

A Roma family at home

Hungarian families are fairly small. Ties with extended family are less important today than in the past. In the cities, families usually live in apartments or single-family homes. Rural families live in small houses.

Since the 1980s, most homes have had electricity and indoor plumbing. In the past, cities had a housing shortage as people moved there for work. However, this problem has lessened as building has grown with the **economy**.

Many Hungarian children attend preschool and kindergarten. Beginning at age six, they study for eight years in primary school. Then, students have several options. They may go to a two-year **vocational** school, a three-year work training school, or a four-year high school.

Children may also choose to attend a gymnasium or a technical training school. Both

Hungarian boys in mathematics class

are four-year high schools. After high school, students may attend one of Hungary's many colleges.

After completing their education, Hungarians join the workforce. Most work in mining, manufacturing, and services. They work to make the economy strong so that Hungary is competitive in the **EU**.

Hungarian society is a mix of **cultures** that have blended together over time. Traditional dress, food, and **folklife** were strong until the mid 1900s. But, forced modernization created many big cultural changes. Today, traditions are mainly seen in folk art and tourist products.

However, food is still a strong tradition. Hungarian dishes often contain meat. One favorite is *gulyás* (GUHL-yahs), a meat stew. Dumplings, potatoes, and noodles are often enjoyed during meals, too.

Paprika is a popular seasoning. A favorite dish that includes paprika is *halászle* (HAHL-ahs-leh), a spicy fish soup. Another is *lecsó* (LEHCH-aw), which is made with paprika, tomatoes, and sausage. For dessert, Hungarians like pastries such as strudel.

Hungarians in traditional clothing

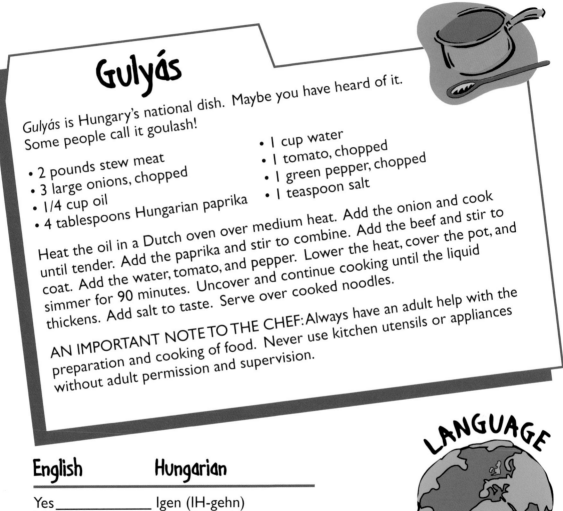

Gulyás

Gulyás is Hungary's national dish. Maybe you have heard of it. Some people call it goulash!

- 2 pounds stew meat
- 3 large onions, chopped
- 1/4 cup oil
- 4 tablespoons Hungarian paprika
- 1 cup water
- 1 tomato, chopped
- 1 green pepper, chopped
- 1 teaspoon salt

Heat the oil in a Dutch oven over medium heat. Add the onion and cook until tender. Add the paprika and stir to combine. Add the beef and stir to coat. Add the water, tomato, and pepper. Lower the heat, cover the pot, and simmer for 90 minutes. Uncover and continue cooking until the liquid thickens. Add salt to taste. Serve over cooked noodles.

AN IMPORTANT NOTE TO THE CHEF: Always have an adult help with the preparation and cooking of food. Never use kitchen utensils or appliances without adult permission and supervision.

LANGUAGE

English	Hungarian
Yes	Igen (IH-gehn)
No	Nem (nehm)
Hello	Szervusztok (SEHR-vuhs-tawk)
Good-bye	Viszontlátásra (VIH-sawnt-lah-tahsh-rah)
Please	Kérem (KAY-rehm)
Thank you	Köszönöm (KUH-suh-nuhm)

Earning a Living

When Hungary was under **communist** rule, the government controlled the **economy**. The nation's **democratic** government has returned control to the people. As a result, the economy has improved.

A Hungarian woman sells produce at a market stand.

Today, most Hungarians work in the service industry. Service fields include education, health care, and engineering. Some Hungarians work in banks or for the Budapest stock exchange. Other people have jobs in trade, where they import and export goods and materials.

About 25 percent of Hungary's people work in mining and manufacturing. Hungarians mine coal, iron, manganese, oil, and natural gas. They also mine bauxite, which is made into alumina. Hungarians manufacture iron, steel, **textiles**, engines, automobiles, electronic goods, and scientific equipment.

During **communist** rule, **economic** growth focused on industry. So today, only 6 percent of Hungarians work in agriculture. Farmers most often grow corn, sugar beets, potatoes, wheat, sunflowers, apples, and plums. They also raise chickens, pigs, cattle, turkeys, and sheep.

Hungary mainly trades with France, Germany, Italy, Russia, and Austria. It exports goods such as alumina, electronics, steel, transportation equipment, fruits, vegetables, meat, and wine. The country imports automobiles, paper, petroleum, electric power, timber, iron ore, and animal feed.

Splendid Cities

Budapest is Hungary's capital and largest city. The Danube River divides the city. Buda is on the west side of the river. Pest is on the east side. Eight bridges connect the two sides.

The capital city is the center of Hungarian **culture**. It is home to many churches, such as the Matthias Church. The Royal Palace still stands in Buda. Pest is home to the House of **Parliament** and the National Gallery.

Budapest also supports many industries with its machine, electrical, and medicine factories. **Textiles** and clothing are made there, too.

Hungary's second-largest city is Debrecen (DEH-breht-sehn). The city was a center for the **Reformation** in Hungary. The Calvinist Great Church still stands in its center square. In the past, Debrecen was an agricultural and trading region. Today, furniture and food are the main industries there. Debrecens also produce machinery and medicines.

Miskolc (MIHSH-kohlts) is Hungary's third-largest city. It is home to much of Hungary's industry. There, the people manufacture machinery, cement, glass, and **textiles**. Many also make wine in the limestone caves in the nearby hills.

Close by, the Avas Calvinist Church has a bell tower that dates to the 1500s. The **Orthodox** church is known for its large picture wall. It is 53 feet (16 m) high and features 88 icons.

In 1872, the village of Óbuda and the cities of Buda and Pest united to form Budapest.

Staying Connected

Under **communism**, the government controlled Hungary's press. Today, Hungarians can communicate more freely. Hungary has about 30 daily newspapers, including *Nepszabadsag*, or "People's Freedom." Many people own televisions. And, more than 3 million Hungarians are connected to the Internet.

Hungarians enjoy freedom to travel, too. In the past, the country's train system was the main form of transportation. By **World War I**, it had become one of the most extensive systems in Europe. Today, the country has about 4,800 miles (7,725 km) of railroad lines.

Since **World War II**, the government has made expanding the roads a priority. Hungary's 99,151 miles (159,568 km) of roadway provide routes for both trade and personal transportation. Since 1980, more Hungarians have been able to own a car. However, buses are the main form of public transportation today.

In Budapest, large accordion buses help Hungarians easily travel the city's 203 square miles (525 sq km).

Hungary's main airport is Ferihegy International Airport in Budapest. Other international airports are FlyBalaton near Lake Balaton and Airport Debrecen in Debrecen. Malev is the country's national airline.

Hungary's Holidays

To celebrate National Day, fireworks light up the sky over Liberty Bridge in Budapest.

Hungary's **culture** changed much with the introduction of **communism**. However, the people were able to hold on to some holidays and festivals to connect them with their past.

On March 15, National Day remembers the beginning of the 1848 revolution and fight for independence. Hungarians also celebrate this as the day its modern **parliament** and **democracy** were created.

International Labor Day is May 1. On this day, Hungarians celebrate the labor movement. Folk dancing and choral singing are part of the festival. Peasant groups often perform these songs and dances.

August 20 is Saint Stephen's day. It celebrates King Stephen I. He became a saint in 1083.

In traditional Easter celebrations, boys throw water on girls!

Republic Day is also a special day. In 1956, the revolution and war for independence began on October 23. And, it is the day the people created the Republic of Hungary in 1989.

Hungarians also celebrate religious holidays. Christmas is traditionally a family time. Village traditions and rituals often take place during Easter. Whitmonday and All Saints' Day are also official holidays in Hungary.

Hungarian Culture

Hungarians have created a distinctive **culture**. It is filled with literature, music, art, sports, and leisure activities.

Hungary has a long literary tradition. In the 1500s, Bálint Balassa wrote the first poetry in the Hungarian language. During the cultural revival in the 1800s, Mihály Csokonai Vitéz (VIH-tayz) wrote fine poetry and plays. József Katona's tragedy *Bánk Bán* was one of the first great Hungarian dramas.

Ferenc Molnár wrote plays, novels, and short stories in the early 1900s. Gyula Illyés (IHL-yaysh), Ferenc Erdei, and others wrote about peasant life in the Discovery of Hungary books in the 1930s.

Peter Esterhazy is an award-winning Hungarian author.

Hungary's musical traditions also began long ago. In the 1500s, Bálint Bakfark was the first Hungarian composer to achieve fame in Europe. And, Franz Liszt (LIHST) was the most celebrated pianist of the 1800s. He wrote piano concertos, symphonies, and many other compositions.

In the 1900s, Béla Bartók (BAHR-tohk) wrote works influenced by Hungarian folk music. He featured the complex harmonies and rhythms in many works, including concertos, string quartets, and an opera.

Hungarians enjoy music and dancing at the Budapest Opera Ball at the State Opera House in Budapest.

Folk music remains a strong part of Hungary's musical tradition. However, the nation's traditional folk arts have all but disappeared. They survive today as commercial products for the tourist industry. However, the people still cherish the great works from the past.

A Hungarian family takes a break from ice-skating together.

Much of Hungary's arts are from the 1900s. Painter László Moholy-Nagy (MAW-hawih-NAHDY) was highly regarded for his experiments in style. He taught at the Bauhaus, an art school in Germany. There, he developed a teaching style that focused on the natural abilities of his students.

Hungarians spend leisure hours visiting theaters and museums. They attend operas and other concerts. They also relax in coffeehouses. The country's warm mineral baths are popular, too.

A Hungarian boy practices the pommel horse. Hungarians have won 13 Olympic medals in gymnastics competition.

In addition, the people often enjoy playing sports, too. Soccer is a favorite, as is tennis. Ice-skating, swimming, boating, and fishing are also popular. Hungarians have won Olympic medals in fencing, swimming, track-and-field, weight lifting, rowing, and wrestling.

Hungary is a beautiful country with a rich **culture**. Today, Hungarians are working to overcome the **economic** challenges of the past. They are looking ahead to a bright future!

Glossary

basin - the entire region of land drained by a river and its tributaries.

communism - a social and economic system in which everything is owned by the government and given to the people as needed. A person who believes in communism is called a communist.

constitution - the laws that govern a country.

culture - the customs, arts, and tools of a nation or people at a certain time.

debate - the formal discussion of a proposal that has been brought before a deliberative body, such as a parliament.

democracy - a governmental system in which the people vote on how to run their country.

deplete - to reduce in number so that effective function is in peril.

dual - having two parts.

economy - the way a nation uses its money, goods, and natural resources.

environment - all the surroundings that affect the growth and well-being of a living thing.

ethnic - of or having to do with a group of people who have the same race, nationality, or culture.

European Union (EU) - an organization of European countries that works toward political, economic, governmental, and social unity.

folklife - the traditions, activities, skills, and products of a particular people or group. Folk art and folk music are part of a country's folklife.

Great Depression - the period from 1929 to 1942 of worldwide economic trouble when there was little buying or selling, and many people could not find work.

habitat - a place where a living thing is naturally found.

highland - elevated or mountainous land.

irrigate - to supply land with water by using channels, streams, and pipes.

League of Nations - an international association created to maintain peace among the nations of the world.

migrate - to move from one place to another, often to find food.

NATO - North Atlantic Treaty Organization. A group formed by the United States, Canada, and some European countries in 1949. It tries to create peace among its nations and protect them from common enemies.

Orthodox - a Christian church that developed from the churches of the Byzantine Empire.

Ottoman Empire - an empire created by Turkish tribes that existed from 1300 to 1922. At its height between the 1600s and 1700s, the empire ruled Europe, northern Africa, and the Arabian Peninsula.

parliament - the highest lawmaking body of some governments.

parliamentary democracy - a form of government in which the decisions of the nation are made by the people through the elected parliament.

principality - a state or a territory ruled by a prince.

Protestant - a Christian who does not belong to the Catholic Church.

rebellion - an armed resistance or defiance of a government. To rebel is to disobey an authority or the government.

Reformation - a religious movement in the 1500s. People who wanted to reform the Catholic Church formed Protestantism by making these changes.

Russian Revolution - two uprisings in 1917, during which the czar of Russia was overthrown and a communist government took over.

textile - a woven fabric or cloth.

vocational - relating to training in a skill or a trade to be pursued as a career.

World War I - from 1914 to 1918, fought in Europe. Great Britain, France, Russia, the United States, and their allies were on one side. Germany, Austria-Hungary, and their allies were on the other side.

World War II - from 1939 to 1945, fought in Europe, Asia, and Africa. Great Britain, France, the United States, the Soviet Union, and their allies were on one side. Germany, Italy, Japan, and their allies were on the other side.

Web Sites

To learn more about Hungary, visit ABDO Publishing Company on the World Wide Web at **www.abdopublishing.com**. Web sites about Hungary are featured on our Book Links page. These links are routinely monitored and updated to provide the most current information available.

Index